# lily of the valley

Charlotte Noonan Mullens

Presentation by *BookLeaf Publishing*

Web: www.bookleafpub.com

E-mail: info@bookleafpub.com

ISBN: 9789357445573

First edition 2022

# DEDICATION

to all of the women who have come before me,
and all of the women who bloom around me.

# ACKNOWLEDGE MENT

I want to express my gratitude to my parents for encouraging a love for reading and writing from a young age. Thank you to Book Leaf Publishing for the opportunity to have my poetry published.

# beneath the soil

first you have to settle in
tie yourself down
bury yourself away
forget the feeling of the sun

first you have wallow in the chill of winter
reach out desperately into nothing
try to recall the glimmer of the stars
empty yourself of the desire to escape

first you have to unravel

# in the night

It finds me in the dead of night
shakes me awake
I hear the flick of the match
as it sets my insides alight

I feel their sharp fingernails scratch me
as they reach in to pluck my nerves
almost as if I were an instrument
they play a diabolical symphony

they leave sharp stones in my stomach
that slice me with every step
I ache more as each minute passes
a scream is trapped inside my head

I have lost count of the times I have been told
this pain is false
a nightmare I cannot wake up from
the only illusion involved is pretending that I am
well
convincing myself I have enough to survive the
day

each night as I lay awake
I lose more of myself to the pain

but each day that I rise
I am reminded I can do it again

# ninety nine years

on the days when my great-grandmother cannot
remember my name or whether she turned the
tap off or whether it is day or night, she talks
about
time, she tells me, goes so quick with a tock and
tick and one minute you're waiting at the theatre
for a boy and next minute it's almost over,
everything is almost gone. time, she says, will
betray

you never think you will rewrite your own
stories and twist your sentences and your
thoughts will scatter like leaves in autumn and
your mind becomes a stranger and

thinking about him makes him feel alive again,
she wears the ring but cannot remember the
wedding dress, calls my father by her first
husband's name and sits across from an empty
place setting, as though she is just waiting for
him to come

home is the bookmark of all her stories: she
remembers the house that she raised her siblings
in, her cousin's house that she was married in

the backyard of, the house she wanted to die in
but no longer owns, she counts them all in the
list of things that she has

lost the address for the pen pal that she never
had the time to write

to see her family have everything she never
could is the deepest knife, it aches in her chest,
reminds her of the way her mother left, leaves
wounds still fresh, despite the

years go by and girls like you, she says, will be
wild and finish school and have jobs and wear
pants and remain unshackled and will put their
elbows on tables and uncross their ankles and
drink straight of bottles and will scream and
shout and argue and play music too loud and
girls like you, she tells me, will have more than
anything a girl like me could get back in my

time is not your friend, she tells me, time will
not answer your letters or come home from the
factory. time will not teach you how to collect
your thoughts or remember your family. time,
she says, goes so quick with a tock and tick and
one moment you have everything and the next
it's gone and you wish it was over. Time has
betrayed me, and I'm sure it will to you too.

# four summers

four summers

one:

you hid your sharpest knife in your silence
severing the threads between us
I pulled relentlessly
desperately hoping it would bring you back to
me

I waited for the smoke to clear
but you became a stranger
your parents smiled at me while I got groceries
there were no answers

I recall that day in december
you were the first person I saw myself in
a flame
equally as vibrant and ferocious and fierce

the girls at school cried over juvenile love
hearts are broken over snapchat and cups of
cheap beer
the love I had lost was gutting
I was alone in the grief I felt

I wrote countless letters I never sent
the words on the page smeared with my tears
I was too proud to admit how much you had
shattered me
the polaroid we took curled into ash in the fire


two:

to make peace with your new friends you spilled
my secrets
shedding the skin of the person you used to be
you poisoned the way that others saw me
what did you want revenge for?

I remembered the weekends spent devouring
sweets
trading second-hand books like a precious
commodity
searching for vintage dresses
sharing canteen money at recess

I clutched on to the sweet memories
every moment soured with the bitterness you
created
everyone asked me where you were
my closest friend no longer exists

I find pieces of you everywhere
the songs we would sing
christmas gifts I adored
I hear your voice in my head

three:

my english tutor lives near you
I almost turn down your street
the ache for what is lost slices through me again
do you ever think of me?

it took hours to put all of the grief into a box
locked away from everything else
I have taught myself to avoid the thoughts
but when I hear your name I still look for you

I wonder what I would do if I saw you again
maybe it is best if we are strangers
the loss still feels raw
I drive past your street

four:

you come back to me in dreams
we grin and giggle as if there are no wounds
a caged bird sings a sweet melody
the pain comes in heavy waves

my twin flame
you extinguished me so furiously
you forced me to discover the beauty in a life
without you
everyday I imagine a world where I had not lost
you

# nine lives

I keep track of the little things I ache for
sandy holidays and long drives
lounging in the sun on a picnic blanket in the
park
ducks scuttling past
singing along at the bar, my friends dressed in
their finest attire
browsing colourful dresses with luscious fabric
sharing canteen food beneath the scorching sun,
our legs sweating on the artificial grass
each day it seems more strange
the way we to used to live

the movies remind me of how it used to be
a warm embrace
I remember looking out at the city lights
glimmer from the balcony
losing myself in a conversation with a stranger
on the train

I recall holding the hand of the elegant italian
woman on the bus
she told me she had to go to the hospital to
switch off her son's life support

it had been less than a year since she had lost the
love of her life
she wore black and her best pearls, a widow
prepared for another funeral
her english was broken but not enough to
disguise her pain
we both shed a tear and turned away
when we reached our stop, she woke me up
she clutched my hand and blessed me, praying
that I will have a beautiful life
a life with as much love that had been given to
her

each week there are more stories
families sob outside the nursing home
their hearts shattered as their loved ones take
their final breath alone
children growing up without seeing their
grandparents
someone losing their strength as they face
another day alone
each day the hope that we can return to what
once was
slips through my fingers like sand

the last time I saw her we watched the news and
drank tea at the nursing home
she asked if there was a virus causing trouble
the year she was born the soldiers came home

carrying the spanish flu with them
she tells me she is moving to a house on the
coast
I'll receive a postcard with her new address to
visit
she says the sea breeze will cure her

I hope with all of my heart that this is just a
season
one life out of nine
maybe there will be another life where we can
hold our families close
another chance at rediscovering everything that
we have lost

# see yourself through the stars

if we are truly made with the remnants of stars

moulded from ether

galaxies in our hearts

it is shameful that we despise ourselves

# the end of everything

open up the sky

let me go to meet the stars

to find my new home

# beauty

we have watched them poison

what it means to be beautiful

until it is something that we don't recognise

yet still ache to be

# sensitive

I have been told to forgive

yet I still carry the knives

that have been plunged in my back

I have been told to leave it all behind

yet I still have dreams

of the snakes whose venom runs in my veins

I have been told to move past what has happened

yet I still ache

for the ones I have lost

I will not apologise for having a tender heart

for only a tender heart

can truly feel the beat of another heart

# reasoning

I write for the women who have been erased by
history

their stories washed away by time

they find me in the depths of my dreams

and urge me to pick up my pen

# towards the sun

absorb everything that is given to you

and make it into your own kind of magic

rebuild your heart

until it can find the sunshine anywhere

# mosaic

I am a mosaic

of all the women I know

shards of their essence

of all their stories

pieces of their radiance

live on within me

# eclipse

gather together all of the joy you can find into a
bouquet

bees hovering over sweet blooming lavender

reading a book with a coffee scented candle

driving at sunrise with the windows down

the warm sand at the beach

let it eclipse all of your pain

your worries

your guilt

let it eclipse the darkest parts of yourself

# how to arrive:

come bearing armfuls of colourful blooms

with baskets of crisp apples and sweet berries

lay down a picnic blanket

and carry the sunshine in your backpack

armed with a fan to swish away the chill of
winter

the scent of blooming lavender will assuage the
pain of the past

and carry us into the next season

# p plates

we get coffee before our sac and sit in the sun to
drink it
thumbing through notes and etching each
sentence into our minds and muscles
the metal benches are scratched with the initials
and profanities
love letters from people long forgotten by the
halls

the universities send out colourful fliers and
powerpoints offering us futures in faraway
towns
we pick our favourites and they become our
dreams
I imagine a life far different from my life now
living alone in a city, studying by the beach
the sun warms my skin and I run my fingers
through the sand

in my nightmares I am in the examination room
my hands paralysed, my mind poisoned
a piercing scream escapes from my mouth
the glass in all of the windows shatter

we wear silly costumes and grin in photos

a mask that weakly disguises our fear of what is
coming
music ring out over the school ground
we drive with our windows down and sing
loudly until there is no air left in our lungs

the next chapter passes in a spin
my body shakes and twitches as I drive
the possibilities of tomorrow seem to rest in the
paper
hiding in between the lines

after it is over
we are through to the other side
it becomes a blur
of silencing the urge to remember it all
teaching myself to breathe deeper

to find joy in more than words and numbers and
scores
searching out in the darkness
to discover what else matters
to find what makes me whole

# return

invest your essence

into finding the person you want to become

all you need

is within yourself

# cathartic

spill yourself out onto the pages

empty out all of your poison

and you will find peace

# kintsugi

in japan they save the lives of their exquisite
pottery after they are shattered

by lining the crevices with liquid gold

turning tragedy into beauty

reframing a break into a rebirth

if only I could learn

to repair my missing pieces

if I could see my wounds

through rose eyes

could I mend what has been lost?

it is proof

that you can restore what is defeated and split

into something remarkable

# in the quiet

in the quiet I found the threads
stitched in me and you
I gave it a little tug
I hope that it went through
in the quiet I heard the wind
she said you send hello
so I told her to send my love
to everyone I know
in the quiet I realised
how many people you can miss
the moments I took for granted
are now a special gift
when this quiet ends
I pray I can still find the threads
to remind me that no matter where we are
we're connected in our heads

# splinters

there is a bike in Washington swallowed by a tree, in a small forest, near the house of the boy who abandoned it. the rusted wheels are in the wooden belly of the tree, and the tree has grown tall around it, the leaves still lush from life. we too, are in the woods, learning to carry something heavy and still grow taller, learning to distance ourselves from the burden. we all have an ache in our stomach we learn to ignore. eventually, they never ask how you live with the growling woods in your belly, but why you still complain of the ache. we all ignore the stones in your stomach, the splinters in our ribcages. we are consumed by the idea of forgetting, of ignoring, instead of becoming who we have to be in the

future is already here before we have time to look back. there is a sea of light in the streets and none it seems to be guiding us home. I ask myself if I still want to see the world if I cannot take a photo, if I can only send postcards and letters and never tell a silent crowd. we forget the past the same way we forget the feeling of the seasons after they are

over and over and over again she comes to me in
dreams, she asks me to forgive her for forgetting
herself. My great grandmother spent my
childhood warning me of the world flying by
before my eyes and I didn't believe her until
now. The nursing home dulls her colours and I
have forgotten how she used to talk when she
told stories, how can I ever soundtrack the music
of her mind when everything is gone with her

forever I will wonder if there is an alternate
universe where the past is never mourned, if in a
parallel all the hours I have spent begging for
time to return are just hours. they are hours I
spent writing a letter to an old friend, a bike ride
around the neighbourhood at sunset, listening to
the wind and there is still so much time I have
left to spend and I listen to the breeze pass
through the

tree that swallowed a bike in the woods of
Washington is testament to living with an ache
inside you, living proof that you can still grow
taller and survive and thrive and rewrite yourself
into something new and different and beautiful,
then who you were before the pain

# lily of the valley

she fights through the winter chill

to reach towards the sun

each bloom is draped with sincerity

and her pollen is brimming with joy

she comes alive in spring

as the leaves emerge again

and the wind whispers of summer's arrival

she is an emblem of may

a taurean beauty

headstrong and wild

a delicate beauty

unperturbed by the world around her